TABLE OF CONTENTS

Synopsis................................... 1 - 2
Pre-Reading Activities........................ 3
Chapters 1 - 5............................. 4 - 5
Chapters 6 - 10............................ 6 - 7
Chapters 11 - 15........................... 8 - 9
Chapters 16 - 21.......................... 10 - 12
Chapters 22 - 27.......................... 13 - 14
Chapters 28 - 31.......................... 15 - 16
Chapters 32 - 36.......................... 17 - 18
Chapters 37 - 47.......................... 19 - 21
Cloze Activity............................... 22
Post-Reading Activities....................... 23
Suggestions For Further Reading.............. 24
Answer Key.............................. 25 - 26

Novel-Ties® are printed on recycled paper.

The purchase of this study guide entitles an individual teacher to reproduce pages for use in a classroom. Reproduction for use in an entire school or school system or for commercial use is prohibited. Beyond the classroom use by an individual teacher, reproduction, transmittal or retrieval of this work is prohibited without written permission from the publisher.

Copyright © 2004, 2020 by LEARNING LINKS

For the Teacher

This reproducible study guide to use in conjunction with the book *There's a Boy in the Girl's Bathroom* consists of lessons for guided reading. Written in chapter-by-chapter format, the guide contains a synopsis, pre-reading activities, vocabulary and comprehension exercises, as well as extension activities to be used as follow-up to the novel.

In a homogeneous classroom, whole class instruction with one title is appropriate. In a heterogeneous classroom, reading groups should be formed: each group works on a different novel on its reading level. Depending upon the length of time devoted to reading in the classroom, each novel, with its guide and accompanying lessons, may be completed in three to six weeks.

Begin using NOVEL-TIES for reading development by distributing the novel and a folder to each child. Distribute duplicated pages of the study guide for students to place in their folders. After examining the cover and glancing through the book, students can participate in several pre-reading activities. Vocabulary questions should be considered prior to reading a chapter; all other work should be done after the chapter has been read. Comprehension questions can be answered orally or in writing. The classroom teacher should determine the amount of work to be assigned, always keeping in mind that readers must be nurtured and that the ultimate goal is encouraging students' love of reading.

The benefits of using NOVEL-TIES are numerous. Students read good literature in the original, rather than in abridged or edited form. The good reading habits, formed by practice in focusing on interpretive comprehension and literary techniques, will be transferred to the books students read independently. Passive readers become active, avid readers.

LEARNING LINKS

THERE'S A BOY IN THE GIRLS' BATHROOM

SYNOPSIS

Bradley Chalkers, who was held back in fourth grade, is now the oldest student in Mrs. Ebbel's fifth-grade class. A known bully with an F-average, he appears to relish his status as a loner and a loser, flaunting his apathy toward school. When a new student, Jeff Fishkin, makes overtures of friendship toward Bradley, it confuses him at first. Soon, however, he decides to enter into a tentative friendship with the new boy.

Bradley also gains an adult friend—Carla Davis, the unconventional new school counselor. With patience and good humor, she helps him address his urge to lie as a way to hide his fear of failure and deny the pain of being an outcast. Miss Davis also helps Jeff with his adjustment as a new student and counsels Colleen, a girl who develops a crush on Jeff after he accidentally enters the girls' bathroom.

When Bradley tries to impress Jeff with his bullying behavior, he ends up getting a black eye from Melinda, one of Colleen's friends. He lies to his parents about the incident, naming Jeff as the person who hit him. Jeff stands by Bradley at first, then suddenly abandons him for a new group of friends, leaving Bradley feeling betrayed and confused. Jeff also resumes acting rudely and stops seeing Miss Davis, claiming he has no need for her counseling.

Throughout the turmoil and confusion, Bradley continues to struggle with the responsibilities of trust and honesty in friendships. He has similar challenges in his family relationships. To escape the mounting tensions at school and at home, Bradley frequently retreats to his bedroom. There he plays with his collection of animal figures, which serve as surrogate friends. Through role-playing with the animals, he releases his true feelings about love and hate.

Although Miss Davis is making progress with Bradley, a group of parents—including Colleen's—are upset with her. They hold a meeting during which they protest against paying a school counselor to advise children, a role they contend is reserved for parents. The group also doesn't agree with Miss Davis' goal of helping students think for themselves.

LEARNING LINKS

Eventually Miss Davis helps Bradley realize that he isn't the monster others say he is. "Bad Bradley" decides to try being "Good Bradley." The experiment works: he gets help from his family to do his homework, discovers the joys of reading, earns a coveted gold star on his book report, and wins back Jeff's friendship. On top of that, he is invited to Colleen's birthday party.

Just as everything seems to be going Bradley's way, he learns that Miss Davis is being transferred to another school. In pain and panic, he expresses hatred toward Miss Davis. She tries to encourage and comfort him, but he rejects her efforts. By the time Bradley relents and seeks her out, she is already gone, having left him an encouraging farewell letter. His response to the letter confirms that his change for the better is well underway. As a final gesture, he sends Miss Davis one of his beloved animal friends.

THERE'S A BOY IN THE GIRLS' BATHROOM

PRE-READING ACTIVITIES AND DISCUSSION QUESTIONS

1. Preview the book by reading the title and the author's name and by looking at the illustration on the cover. What do you think this book will be about? Do you think this book will be serious or humorous? Have you read any other books by Louis Sachar?

2. Read the first paragraph of *There's a Boy in the Girls' Bathroom.* What does Bradley's seat in his classroom reveal about him? What does it tell about the way others judge him? Do you think that you would want Bradley as a friend? Why or why not?

3. What problems do you face when you try to make new friends? What problems does a new student in your school face? As you read *There's a Boy in the Girls' Bathroom*, think about your answers to these questions. Think about how the characters deal with these problems.

4. A person's reputation refers to the way someone is regarded in a particular community. It could be a reputation at school, in the town, or among those who are the same age. How important is it to have a good reputation? Once someone has a reputation, how easy or difficult is it to change that reputation?

5. Have you ever failed to stand up for someone who was your friend? If you faced the same situation again, would you act in the same way? Do you think friends should always stand up for each other? If not, when is it all right *not* to support your friends?

6. What is a bully? Have you ever faced a bully? Why do you think some people become bullies? Do you think people become bullies by choice? If not, how might they try to change? How might others make it hard for them to change?

7. Is there a guidance counselor in your school? Why would some students visit a guidance counselor? Why might it sometimes be easier to discuss a problem with a guidance counselor than with a family member or friend? What qualities should a counselor have to gain your trust?

THERE'S A BOY IN THE GIRLS' BATHROOM

CHAPTERS 1 – 5

Vocabulary: Draw a line from each word on the left to its definition on the right. Then use the numbered words to fill in the blanks in the sentences below.

1. distorted   a. stunned or shocked
2. strewn   b. laughed in a way that showed lack of respect
3. snickered   c. bent or twisted out of shape
4. fluttered   d. willing to let something happen or exist
5. flabbergasted   e. having a powerful effect
6. tolerate   f. scattered over a large area in a messy way
7. drastic   g. moved gently in quick, wavy motions

. . . .

1. The students were _____ when the clown removed his makeup and revealed that he was the principal.

2. We should _____ the differences in each other that make us special.

3. The curtains _____ in the breeze.

4. The burglar _____ at the police officer as he escaped out the back door.

5. After the tornado passed, pieces of the building were _____ all over the land.

6. Moving from the jungle to the zoo was a _____ change for the gorilla.

7. The plastic fork was _____ by the heat of the flames before it finally melted in the campfire.

Read to find out why Bradley's teacher thinks he needs the help of the new counselor.

LEARNING LINKS 4

Chapters 1 – 5 (cont.)

Questions:

1. How did Mrs. Ebbel reveal her low expectations for Bradley?
2. How did Bradley show his displeasure with school?
3. How did Jeff's behavior surprise Bradley? How did Jeff's behavior confuse Bradley?
4. What role did the toy animals play in Bradley's life?
5. How did Bradley try to prevent his mother from going to the parent-teacher conference?

Questions for Discussion:

1. In your opinion, is there anything Mrs. Ebbel could do to help Bradley?
2. Do you think Bradley's parents might help their son?
3. Why do you think Jeff wanted Bradley as a friend?
4. Do you think Miss Davis will be able to help Bradley?
5. Do you know anyone who behaves like Bradley? Why do you think this person acts that way?

Literary Device: Metaphor

A metaphor is a figure of speech in which a comparison between two unlike objects is suggested or implied. This is an example of a metaphor from the first paragraph of the book:

> He [Bradley] was an island.

What is being compared?

_____

What does this reveal about Bradley?

_____

_____

_____

Writing Activities:

1. Write a journal entry about a time when you or someone you know told a lie. Tell whether the lie got the person into trouble.
2. Imagine you are Bradley and write a letter to one of your animal friends expressing your thoughts and feelings as you wait for your mother to return from the parent-teacher conference.

THERE'S A BOY IN THE GIRLS' BATHROOM

CHAPTER 6 – 10

Vocabulary: Use the context to determine the meaning of the underlined word in each of the following sentences. Then draw a line from each word on the left to its meaning on the right.

- My bedroom became so <u>cluttered</u>, I could no longer find anything I needed.
- The little boy called <u>frantically</u> for his cat until the firefighters were able to rescue it.
- I <u>grimaced</u> as I scraped gum off the under side of my desk.
- Growling <u>ferociously</u>, the lion clawed at the bars of his cage.
- She <u>blushed</u> as she accepted the award in front of all her classmates.
- The beagle puppy <u>squirmed</u> inside the carrier, which had become too small for him.
- "I'm proud to be a Native American!" <u>declared</u> Snowhawk.

1. cluttered
2. frantically
3. grimaced
4. ferociously
5. blushed
6. squirmed
7. declared

a. made a twisted face showing pain or disgust
b. with crazy fear or worry
c. stated plainly and firmly
d. filled with an untidy collection of objects
e. wiggled with discomfort or shame
f. with wild force
g. turned red in the face with shame or shyness

> Read to find out how Miss Davis influenced Bradley and Jeff.

Questions:

1. Why did Jeff walk into the girls' bathroom?
2. How did Miss Davis help Jeff to relax and trust her?
3. Why did Miss Davis advise Jeff to be nice, honest, and friendly to Bradley?
4. Why did Bradley think Miss Davis was tricking him during their meeting?
5. Why did Bradley refuse to let Miss Davis hang his picture on her wall?
6. How were Bradley's feelings about Jeff changing? How do you know this?

Questions for Discussion:

1. Do you think it is wise for a teacher or school counselor to be on a first-name basis with students?
2. Why do you think that Bradley behaved as though he didn't want to sit with Jeff in the cafeteria?

LEARNING LINKS

Chapter 6 – 10 (cont.)

3. What do you think a teacher, such as Miss Davis, could learn from a student?
4. In your opinion, why did Miss Davis behave as though she accepted everything Bradley said as the truth?
5. In what ways do you think Bradley was not fulfilling Jeff's needs in a friend?
6. Do you agree with Miss Davis that there are no accidents?

Literary Device: Simile

A simile is a figure of speech in which a comparison is made between two unlike objects using the words "like" or "as." For example:

> He backed away from it [Miss Davis' hand] as if it were some kind of poisonous snake.

What is being compared?

_____

What does this reveal about Bradley's feelings for Miss Davis?

_____
_____

Literary Element: Characterization

Compare Bradley and Jeff in a Venn diagram such as the one below. Write the characteristics they have in common in the overlapping parts of the circle. Add information as you continue to read the novel.

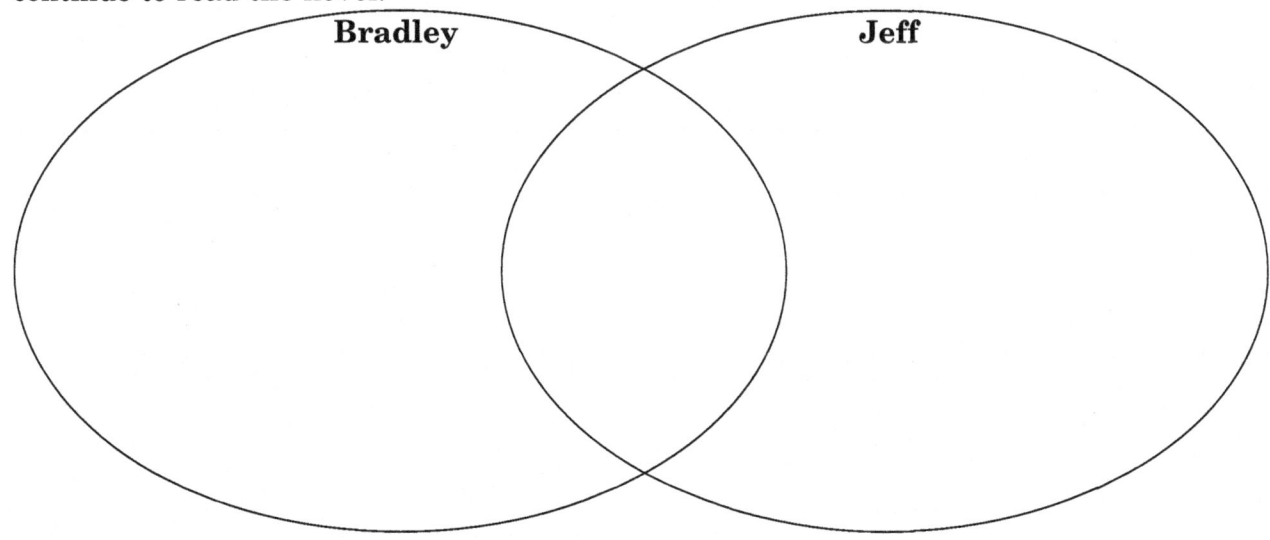

Bradley   **Jeff**

Writing Activity:

Imagine you are Jeff and write a journal entry describing your mixed feelings about your growing friendship with Bradley.

CHAPTERS 11 – 15

Vocabulary: Use a word from the Word Box to replace the underlined word or phrase in each of the following sentences. Write the word on the line below the sentences.

> *WORD BOX*
> anguish   hysterically   reluctantly   timidly
> hesitated   massive   sneered

1. The pyramids in Egypt are built of <u>huge</u> stone blocks.
   _____

2. <u>Not wanting to</u>, my brother picked up the shovel and went outside to scoop snow from our driveway.
   _____

3. Throughout the entire roller coaster ride, the girl behind me screamed <u>uncontrollably</u>.
   _____

4. He was in <u>great emotional pain</u> over the suffering of the injured bird.
   _____

5. Staring at her feet, she <u>shyly</u> took the hand of her dancing partner.
   _____

6. I <u>paused with doubt</u> before opening the door to the gloomy mansion.
   _____

7. She <u>raised her lip in an expression of disrespect</u> when I pulled on my sweater, which was old and full of holes.
   _____

> Read to find out why Bradley is beaten up.

Questions:

1. In what ways did Jeff try to gain Bradley's approval?
2. What evidence showed that Jeff would like to befriend others beside Bradley?
3. Why did Colleen want Miss Davis to solve her problem for her?
4. Why didn't Bradley ever get to Jeff's house to do homework?
5. How did Bradley try to restore his pride when he returned home after being beaten?

Chapters 11 – 15 (cont.)

Questions for Discussion:

1. Miss Davis said that "friendships are stronger when everyone has different opinions to share." Do your friends make it easy or hard to share differing opinions?
2. Do you think it is right to want your best friend to be friends only with you? Can a friendship survive as a totally exclusive arrangement?
3. Do you think students should have to get permission from their parents to talk to a counselor?
4. Why do you think Bradley's mother believed her son's story?
5. What do you think will happen as a result of Mrs. Chalkers' call to the school?

Readers' Theater:

Work with two of your classmates to prepare Chapter Eleven as a readers' theater presentation. One person should read the part of Bradley, another should read the part of Jeff, and a third person should read the girls' parts and the connecting narration. Practice reading your parts to develop greater fluency and realistic expression. You may use simple props or articles of clothing to identify the setting and the characters.

Writing Activity:

Imagine that you are Mrs. Chalkers and write a letter to the school principal complaining about the way that Bradley was bullied by other students. Then write a response to that letter from the principal to Mrs. Chalkers.

THERE'S A BOY IN THE GIRLS' BATHROOM

CHAPTERS 16 – 21

Vocabulary: Use the context to determine the meaning of the underlined word in each of the following sentences. Then compare your definition with a dictionary definition.

1. The barking of the neighbor's new dog is <u>terrorizing</u> our cat.

    Your definition _____

    Dictionary definition _____

2. He <u>pried</u> the lid off the can of paint.

    Your definition _____

    Dictionary definition _____

3. I <u>beamed</u> when I opened my present and saw the computer that I had wanted for a long time.

    Your definition _____

    Dictionary definition _____

4. The high <u>quality</u> of service at the auto garage keeps the customers happy.

    Your definition _____

    Dictionary definition _____

5. The bakery clerk ordered a large <u>quantity</u> of flour each month.

    Your definition _____

    Dictionary definition _____

6. The nervous little bird <u>darted</u> from branch to branch.

    Your definition _____

    Dictionary definition _____

7. My sister has so much <u>confidence</u> in herself that she never says, "I can't."

    Your definition _____

    Dictionary definition _____

> Read to find out what happens to Jeff and Bradley's friendship.

LEARNING LINKS

Chapters 16 – 21 (cont.)

Questions:

1. Why was Jeff called into the principal's office?

2. Why did Jeff refer to Bradley as his best friend even after his meeting with the principal?

3. Why did the boys who were playing basketball invite Jeff to join them?

4. How did Bradley cheer himself up after Jeff rejected him?

5. Why did Jeff decide to stop visiting Miss Davis?

6. How did Miss Davis learn that Jeff hadn't given Bradley the black eye?

7. Why did Miss Davis tell Bradley he was very brave as their meeting came to an end?

Questions for Discussion:

1. Do you think it is possible for Bradley's parents to have as little understanding of their child as they seemed to have?

2. Why do you think Melinda didn't want anyone to know she gave Bradley the black eye?

3. Why do you think Jeff gave up his friendship with Bradley so quickly and easily?

4. What temporary personality change do you think Bradley revealed when he asked Jeff to do homework with him?

5. Did you feel sorry for Bradley when Jeff made new friends? Did you feel angry with Jeff for the way he treated Bradley? Or do you think Bradley deserved to be shunned?

6. Why do you think Bradley returned to his former hateful attitude?

7. What do you think would need to happen before Bradley could trust anyone again?

8. Do you agree with Miss Davis that Bradley had a fear of failure? Do you or anyone you know have a similar fear? Why might some people have a fear of success?

9. Miss Davis says that when you tell a lie, the only person you're lying to is yourself. What do you think she means?

THERE'S A BOY IN THE GIRLS' BATHROOM

Chapters 16 – 21 (cont.)

Literary Element: Conflict

A conflict is a struggle between opposing forces. An external conflict is a character's struggle against an outside force, such as nature, fate, or another person. An internal conflict is a personal struggle that takes place within a character's mind. What external conflicts has Bradley faced so far?

_____

_____

What is one of Bradley's internal conflicts?

_____

_____

Literary Device: Foreshadowing

Foreshadowing refers to the clues an author provides to suggest what will take place later in the story.

How was Jeff's rejection of Bradley foreshadowed?

_____

_____

What might the reaction of Colleen's parents foreshadow for Miss Davis?

_____

_____

Writing Activities:

1. Write about a time when you had a conflict with one of your friends. What led to the conflict? How did you deal with it? What did you learn from the experience?

2. Write a short poem describing the pain Bradley must feel about what Jeff did to him. In your poem, try to use a metaphor or a simile.

THERE'S A BOY IN THE GIRLS' BATHROOM

CHAPTERS 22 – 27

Vocabulary: Synonyms are words with similar meanings. Draw a line from each word in Column A to its synonym in Column B. Then use the words in Column A to fill in the blanks in the sentences below.

1. scoffed   a. waved
2. anticipation   b. real
3. flailed   c. thoughtful
4. considerate   d. gleamed
5. befuddled   e. mocked
6. genuine   f. puzzled
7. glistened   g. expectation

．．．

1. The raindrops on the rose petals _____ in the sunshine.

2. Trying to get our attention, he _____ his arms over his head.

3. The directions were so complicated, we felt _____ even before the game began.

4. Experts at the museum convinced me that the sword was not a fake, but a(n) _____ weapon used in the Civil War.

5. When we brought cool lemonade to the gardeners working on a hot summer day, they thanked us for being so _____.

6. The professional carpenter _____ at my attempt to build a simple bookcase.

7. Jason licked his lips with _____ when he saw the freshly baked cookies.

> Read to find out why Bradley goes into the girls' bathroom.

Questions:

1. Why did Bradley begin to concentrate in class?

2. Why did Bradley throw away his list?

3. Why did the girls attack Jeff?

LEARNING LINKS

Chapters 22 – 27 (cont.)

4. Why did Bradley give up in his attempt to get a gold star?
5. Why did Bradley dash into the girls' bathroom?

Questions for Discussion:

1. What personality traits do you think Bradley's list revealed? What topics would you write in a list?
2. What lesson do you think Miss Davis was trying to teach Bradley when she discussed monsters with him?
3. In your opinion, why did Bradley finally shake hands with Miss Davis?
4. Why do you think Jeff was rude to the girls?
5. Why did Bradley find it so difficult to change his reputation? What do you think would have to happen before people would stop seeing him as a "monster"?
6. In what ways do you think Bradley and Jeff have changed places?
7. In what ways do you think Bradley's visit with Miss Davis was different from all former visits? What did this reveal about Bradley?

Literary Device: Simile

What is being compared in the following simile?

> Bradley ran at them [the boys]. They scattered and regrouped, like pigeons.

How does this simile help you picture the scene?

Writing Activity:

Imagine you are Miss Davis and write a progress report on Bradley Chalkers. Tell about the ways that he has already changed and how you hope he will continue to change in the future.

THERE'S A BOY IN THE GIRLS' BATHROOM

CHAPTERS 28 – 31

Vocabulary: Use the context to help you choose the best definition for the underlined word in each of the following sentences. Circle the letter of the word or phrase you choose.

1. I have to <u>concentrate</u> when I'm docking my boat in the crowded harbor.
   a. stand still   b. call out loudly   c. breathe deeply   d. pay close attention

2. With <u>disgust</u>, she scraped the slimy mud from her shoes.
   a. force   b. dislike   c. pride   d. joy

3. The kitten circled the box <u>inquisitively</u> before crawling inside.
   a. playfully   b. angrily   c. curiously   d. quietly

4. I stared in <u>disbelief</u> as a hawk swooped down and carried off my straw hat from where it hung on the fence post.
   a. pain   b. delight   c. fear   d. wonder

5. The thunder crashed, and the lights <u>abruptly</u> went out.
   a. suddenly   b. finally   c. slowly   d. rudely

6. She <u>fumbled</u> in her drawer for the earring, but it kept slipping out of her grasp.
   a. moved clumsily   b. explored carefully   c. searched roughly   d. looked nervously

7. I'm <u>baffled</u> when someone tells me they actually enjoy cleaning.
   a. puzzled   b. sad   c. annoyed   d. sorry

Read to find out what happens when Bradley decides to do his homework.

Questions:

1. Why did Bradley try to do his homework?
2. Why did Bradley hesitate to ask his family members to help him with his homework?
3. Why did Bradley regret that he and his father completed his homework quickly?

Chapters 28 – 31 (cont.)

4. Why didn't Bradley hand in his completed math homework?
5. How did you know that Bradley would try doing his homework again?
6. Why did Bradley's mother decide not to attend the Concerned Parents Organization meeting?

Questions for Discussion:

1. Why do you think Bradley now referred to Miss Davis as Carla?
2. What do you think Bradley learned about his family when he asked them for help with his homework? What do you think they learned about him?
3. Why do you think Bradley became so nervous about handing in his homework? What did he fear?
4. Do you think Bradley's mother should go to the meeting about Miss Davis? If so, what might she say to the Concerned Parents Organization?

Literary Device: Foreshadowing

What might the Concerned Parents Organization meeting foreshadow?

_____

_____

Writing Activity:

Write a letter to Bradley encouraging him to continue his efforts to be the "Good Bradley" rather than the "Bad Bradley." Offer suggestions to him about how he can improve his image.

THERE'S A BOY IN THE GIRLS' BATHROOM

CHAPTERS 32 – 36

Vocabulary: Use a word from the Word Box to replace the underlined word or phrase in each of the following sentences. Write the word you choose on the line below the sentence.

> *WORD BOX*
> awkwardly   dumbfounded
> defiantly   overwhelmed
> determination

1. Grandpa is <u>weighed down</u> by all the things he needs to fix in his old house.
   _____

2. With <u>a strong sense of purpose</u>, she marched out to weed the overgrown garden.
   _____

3. "I will not be kicked out of my own room!" Tara shouted <u>boldly</u>.
   _____

4. He was <u>completely surprised</u> when he discovered he had won the grand prize.
   _____

5. Our dog walks <u>in a clumsy way</u> because of the cast on his broken leg.
   _____

> Read to find out about a drastic change in Bradley's attitude.

Questions:
1. Why did Bradley think Miss Davis's book was his lucky charm?
2. Why did the boys invite Bradley to play basketball with them?
3. Why did Jeff think life was weird?
4. Why did Bradley forget everything his father taught him about dribbling a basketball?
5. Why did Bradley's father let him go on reading past his bed time?
6. Why was Bradley worried about going to the party?

Chapters 32 – 36 (cont.)

Questions for Discussion:

1. Why do you think Miss Davis didn't laugh when Bradley teased her about going to the principal's office?

2. Why was Bradley now able to be friendly to the boys and accept their teasing?

3. Why do you think Colleen came to see Miss Davis even though she "wasn't supposed to"?

4. Do you think that Bradley's positive attitude was responsible for his acceptance by others, or did Carla's book have magic properties?

5. At first, Bradley didn't want to tell Miss Davis about all the good things that were happening to him. Why do you think he felt that way? Why do you think he suddenly shared his good news with her?

Writing Activities:

1. Have you ever had what you considered to be a "lucky charm"? What was it? Why did you believe it was lucky? Write a paragraph describing your lucky charm. Write a second paragraph about the luck it seemed to bring you. Write a final paragraph telling how you feel about the lucky charm today.

2. Imagine that you are paying a visit to Carla Davis. Write the dialogue that you might have with her, describing a problem you face.

THERE'S A BOY IN THE GIRLS' BATHROOM

CHAPTERS 37 – 47

Vocabulary: In the following chart, write "A" or "S" to indicate whether the words in each word pair are synonyms or antonyms. Then use a word from the chart to fill in a blank in each of the sentences below.

		A/S
1.	justified – wrong	
2.	conclusion – beginning	
3.	essence – spirit	
4.	throbbed – pulsed	
5.	bizarre – ordinary	
6.	swerved – veered	
7.	sternly – kindly	
8.	scowled – grinned	

1. The car _____ sharply to the right to avoid hitting the pothole in the middle of the road.

2. The actress wore such a(n) _____ costume to the award ceremony that people stared at her all night.

3. Flying the American flag captures the _____ of the Fourth of July holiday.

4. The _____ of the film was so sad that all the people left the theater with tears in their eyes.

5. The judge _____ warned the jurors not to discuss the case outside the courtroom.

6. My hard work seemed to be _____ when I received a medal for my performance.

7. Waiting to go onstage, my heart _____ as I stood in the wings.

8. I _____ at my little sister when she destroyed my homework.

Read to find out what happens at the meeting of the Concerned Parents Organization.

Chapters 37 – 47 (cont.)

Questions:

1. Why were the parents who came to the meeting critical of Miss Davis?
2. Why did Bradley rip up his book report?
3. How did Bradley receive a gold star? Why didn't he appreciate it?
4. Why did Bradley try to write a letter to Carla?
5. How did Jeff prepare Bradley for the birthday party?
6. What evidence showed that Bradley's experience at the birthday party had been successful?
7. How did Bradley's letter reveal Carla's good influence on him?

Questions for Discussion:

1. Do you think Bradley's mother should have attended the meeting?
2. Do you agree with Miss Davis that schools should teach children *how* to think, rather than *what* to think?
3. Do you think Bradley's parents might have been more helpful to their son when he was suffering over Carla's departure?
4. Do you think Carla might have done more for Bradley to soften the blow of her leaving?
5. Do you think Carla could have done anything to ensure that she would stay at Bradley's school?
6. Do you think that schools should have counselors?
7. Why do you think the author ended the story with a question about whether Bradley was smiling or frowning?

Literary Device: Symbolism

A symbol in literature is an object, person, or event that represents an idea or a set of ideas. What does Bradley's gift of Ronnie to Carla symbolize?

_____

_____

_____

Chapters 37 – 47 (cont.)

Literary Elements:

I. *Characterization* — Use the chart below to compare Bradley at the beginning of the novel to Bradley at the end of the novel. Discuss with your classmates how Bradley changed.

Bradley at the Beginning	Bradley at the End

II. *Theme* — The theme of a novel refers to the author's message or its central idea. Consider what the novel is saying about the following topics and create a list of themes for *There's a Boy in the Girls' Bathroom*.

- friendship
- advice
- peer pressure
- family
- change
- lying
- love
- learning

Writing Activities:

Imagine that you are Miss Davis. Write a letter to Bradley in reply to his letter at the end of the book. Include details from Miss Davis's new job as a kindergarten teacher.

THERE'S A BOY IN THE GIRLS' BATHROOM

CLOZE ACTIVITY

The following passage has been taken from Chapter Twenty-nine of the novel. Read it through completely and then fill in each blank with a word that makes sense. Afterwards you may compare your language with that of the author.

It was almost time for school to start. *What if I have to put it* [homework] *on her _____1 before the bell rings or it doesn't _____?*2 He fumbled through his book for his _____,3 stood up, then headed for Mrs. Ebbel's desk.

_____4 became more nervous with each step he _____.5 His mouth was dry and he had _____6 breathing. He could hardly see where he _____7 going. He felt like he was going _____8 faint. Mrs. Ebbel's desk seemed so far away. _____9 was like he was looking at it _____10 the wrong end of a telescope. His _____11 pounded and his homework rattled in his _____.12

Somehow he made it to her desk _____13 tried to focus on the sheets of _____14 the other kids had put there. It _____15 like arithmetic homework! Page 43!

But instead _____16 feeling better, he felt worse—like he _____17 going to explode.

"Do you want something, _____?"18 asked Mrs. Ebbel.

He looked at his homework _____19 in his hand. Then he tore it _____20 half and dropped it in the wastepaper _____21 next to Mrs. Ebbel's desk.

He instantly felt _____.22 His head cleared and his breathing returned _____23 normal. His heart stopped pounding.

He walked _____24 to his desk, took a deep breath, _____,25 and sat down. He folded his arms _____26 his desktop and lay his head down _____27 across them. He felt sad, but relieved, as he gazed at the gold stars.

LEARNING LINKS 22

THERE'S A BOY IN THE GIRLS' BATHROOM

POST-READING ACTIVITIES AND DISCUSSION QUESTIONS

1. **Literature Circle:** Have a literature circle discussion in which you tell your personal reactions to *There's a Boy in the Girls' Bathroom*. Here are some questions and sentence starters to help your literature circle begin a discussion.
    - How are you like Bradley? How are you different?
    - Do you find the characters in the novel realistic? Why or why not?
    - Which character did you like the most? The least?
    - Who else would you like to have read this novel? Why?
    - What questions would you like to ask the author about this novel?
    - It is not fair when . . .
    - I didn't understand why . . .
    - Bradley learned that . . .

2. **Pair/Share:** Select a passage from the book that you found powerful or meaningful in relation to your own life. Rehearse reading this passage before reading it aloud to a partner. Discuss why this passage is important. Then listen to the passage your partner has selected and discuss the importance of this selection.

3. **Readers' Theater:** It is fun to read a story with dialogue as though it were a play. Select a chapter (other than Chapter Eleven if you have done it already) with lots of dialogue and several different characters. One student can read the narration. The other students read the words of their characters that appear inside the quotation marks. Ignore phrases such as "he said" or "she said." You may want to use simple props to distinguish characters and establish setting. Present this chapter to the rest of your class.

4. Imagine that this book is going to be made into a movie. Who do you think should play the roles of Bradley, Jeffrey, Carla, and Mr. and Mrs. Chalkers? Should any scenes be changed, left out, or added? What scenes do you think will work best in a film version. Is there any music that you would suggest to use as background for parts of the film?

5. Create a book cover for *There's a Boy in the Girls' Bathroom*. On the front cover, create an illustration that shows an important incident in the story, and write the book title and author's name. On the back cover, write a short paragraph that tells a little bit about the story and encourages people to read the book.

SUGGESTIONS FOR FURTHER READING

* Applegate, Katherine *The One and Only Ivan*. HarperCollins.
* Blume, Judy. *Tales of a Fourth Grade Nothing*. Puffin.
* Clements, Andrew. *Frindle*. Antheneum.
    _____. *Trouble Maker*. Antheneum.
  Craft, Jerry. *New Kid*. Quill Tree.
* Danziger, Paula. *The Cat Ate My Gymsuit*. Puffin.
  DeClements, Barthe. *Sixth Grade Can Really Kill You*. Scholastic.
  Hahn, Mary Downing. *Stepping on the Cracks*. HMH Books.
* Hiaason, Carl. *Hoot*. Ember.
* Namioka, Lensey. *Yang the Youngest and his Terrible Ear*. Yearling.
* Spinelli, Jerry. *Crash*. Yearling.
* _____. *Stargirl*. Ember.
  Yep, Laurence. *The Lost Garden*. HarperCollins.

Some Other Books by Louis Sachar

  The Boy Who Lost His Face. Yearling.
  Fuzzy Mud. Yearling.
* *Holes*. Yearling.
  Sideways Stories from Wayside School. HarperCollins.
  Sixth Grade Secrets. Scholastic.
* *Small Steps*. Ember.

* NOVEL-TIES Study Guides are available for these titles.

ANSWER KEY

Chapters 1 – 5
Vocabulary: 1. c 2. f 3. b 4. g 5. a 6. d 7. e; 1. flabbergasted 2. tolerate 3. fluttered 4. snickered 5. strewn 6. drastic 7. distorted

Questions: 1. Mrs. Ebbel revealed her low expectations for Bradley by seating him in the back of the classroom, apologizing for seating the new student next to him, and by showing no concern for Bradley's failing grades. 2. Bradley showed his displeasure with school by scribbling during lessons, making faces at the new student, and by cutting his failing test papers into small pieces. 3. Bradley was surprised that Jeff made overtures of friendship toward him, and Jeff didn't tell the teacher that Bradley had cheated him out of a dollar. Although Bradley could accept the hatred of his classmates, he was confused and couldn't immediately accept Jeff's kindness. 4. The toy animals were Bradley's imaginary friends who were substitutes for the real friends that he lacked. 5. Bradley tried to prevent his mother from going to the parent-teacher conference by lying and telling her she had promised to take him to the zoo.

Chapters 6 – 10
Vocabulary: 1. d 2. b 3. a 4. f 5. g 6. e 7. c

Questions: 1. As a new student in the school, Jeff got lost trying to find the counselor's office and entered the girls' bathroom by mistake. 2. Miss Davis helped Jeff to relax and trust her by admitting that she, too, suffered from being new to the school: she was scared of getting lost, and worried about making new friends. She told Jeff they could be on a first-name basis and she promised to keep their conversations confidential. 3. Miss Davis advised Jeff to be nice, honest, and friendly to Bradley because she thought it would engender the same kind of behavior in return. 4. Bradley thought he was being tricked when Miss Davis responded in unexpected ways to his behavior. Instead of getting angry at his rude comments or questioning his lies, she seemed pleased with what he said. 5. Since Bradley rarely received praise for his work, he was accustomed to people being rude to him at school, which caused him to be rude in return. He didn't know how to react to kindness, so he responded in his usual rude manner, refusing to let Miss Davis hang his picture on the wall. 6. Bradley revealed his pleasure with having Jeff as a friend by no longer ignoring him and willingly spending time with him at recess. He was willing to make conversation with Jeff and even plan mischievous activities for the two of them.

Chapters 11 – 15
Vocabulary: 1. huge–massive 2. not wanting to–reluctantly 3. uncontrollably–hysterically 4. great emotional pain–anguish 5. shyly–timidly 6. paused with doubt–hesitated 7. raised her lip, etc.–sneered

Questions: 1. In order to gain Bradley's approval, Jeff agreed to behave in an uncharacteristic manner by taking Bradley into the girls' bathroom and lying that he hated girls, too. He also suggested that he disliked Miss Davis, just to make Bradley believe that friends thought alike. 2. When Jeff tossed the ball right back to the boys playing basketball and when he refused to be rude to the girls, it was clear that he would like to have befriended others in his class beside Bradley. 3. Colleen wanted Miss Davis to solve the problem of whom to invite to her birthday party. If she invited Bradley as well as Jeff, people might not come: if she didn't invite Bradley, Jeff might not come. 4. Bradley never got to Jeff's house to do homework because he was too humiliated when the girls he tried to bully fought back successfully. 5. To restore his pride, Bradley told his mother and sister that he had been bullied by a gang. He blamed Jeff for being the leader of the gang.

Chapters 16 – 21
Vocabulary: 1. terrorizing–causing extreme fear 2. pried–raised, moved, or forced open with a lever 3. beamed–smiled broadly 4. quality–excellence or value 5. quantity–amount or number 6. darted–moved suddenly and quickly 7. confidence–trust or faith in a person or thing

Questions: 1. Jeff was called into the principal's office because Mr. Chalkers had reported that Jeff had given his son a black eye. 2. Jeff still thought Bradley was his best friend because he was unaware that Bradley had falsely identified him as the assailant. 3. Jeff was asked to join the basketball game because the boys were impressed by Jeff who they thought had given Bradley a black eye. 4. Bradley cheered himself up by pretending that his toy animals welcomed him home. 5. Jeff decided to stop visiting Miss Davis because he claimed all his problems were solved when he gave Bradley a black eye and acquired eight new friends. 6. Miss Davis learned that Jeff had not given Bradley the black eye when Colleen revealed that Melinda was the assailant. 7. Miss Davis told Bradley he was brave because she wanted to play along with his assertion that he would die if he discussed school. She wanted to compliment Bradley for saying as much as he did and wanted him to feel able to return.

THERE'S A BOY IN THE GIRLS' BATHROOM

Chapters 22 – 27
Vocabulary: 1. e 2. g 3. a 4. c 5. f 6. b 7. d; 1. glistened 2. flailed 3. befuddled 4. genuine 5. considerate 6. scoffed 7. anticipation
Questions: 1. Bradley began to concentrate because he was determined to come up with a long list of topics to discuss with Miss Davis so that they would not have to discuss school again. 2. Bradley threw away his list because his sister criticized it and claimed that it was inappropriate. 3. The girls attacked Jeff in response to his unexpected rudeness. 4. Bradley gave up in his attempt to get a gold star because his day at school had been a total disappointment. After Jeff accused him of giving him a black eye, the rest of the boys taunted him and threatened to beat him up. Unable to overcome his bad reputation and nervous about the violence and betrayal he faced, Bradley knew he could not receive a gold star. 5. Bradley dashed into the girls' bathroom to avoid the gang of boys who threatened to beat him up.

Chapters 28 – 31
Vocabulary: 1. d 2. b 3. c 4. d 5. a 6. a 7. a
Questions: 1. Bradley tried to do his homework to please Miss Davis. 2. Bradley hesitated to ask his family members for help because he assumed they would mistake his motives and not take him seriously. 3. Bradley was enjoying working with his father so much, that he regretted when they finished quickly. This was the first time that they had interacted successfully, each pleased with the other. 4. Bradley became so anxiety-ridden when it was time to hand in his homework, that he sought relief from his mental anguish by tearing up the paper and throwing it away. 5. It was clear that Bradley would try doing homework again when he borrowed a book from Carla to fulfill a book report assignment. 6. Bradley's mother decided not to attend the meeting that the Concerned Parents Organization was holding to discuss Miss Davis because she and her son had no complaints about her. Therefore, she thought she did not need to be there.

Chapters 32 – 36
Vocabulary: 1. weighed down–overwhelmed 2. strong sense of purpose–determination 3. boldly—defiantly 4. completely surprised–dumbfounded 5. in a clumsy way–awkwardly
Questions: 1. Bradley thought Miss Davis's book was his lucky charm because he had difficulty believing he was responsible for the librarian's compliments, his teacher's trust, his success at basketball, and the invitation to Colleen's party. 2. The boys invited Bradley to play basketball because they were responding positively in response to Bradley's new positive attitude. Instead of meeting Jeff's challenge with hostility, he greeted him amiably. 3. Jeff reflected that life was odd when he noticed that Bradley was reading and that he had developed a more positive attitude. He also found it strange that Colleen entered the boys' bathroom when he was in there because at one time he had made a similar mistake. 4. Bradley was so happy, surprised, and confused when Colleen asked him to her party, that he forgot how to dribble. 5. Bradley's father was so pleased to find Bradley reading that he allowed him to break a rule and continue reading past his bed time. 6. Having never before been invited to a party by his peers, Bradley worried that he would embarrass himself by doing something inappropriate.

Chapters 37 – 47
Vocabulary: 1. A 2. A 3. S 4. S 5. A 6. S 7. A 8. A; 1. swerved or veered 2. bizarre 3. essence or spirit 4. conclusion 5. sternly 6. justified 7. throbbed or pulsed 8. scowled
Questions: 1. The parents who came to the meeting were critical of spending public money on a counselor, who they thought was worthless. They also thought Miss Davis should have provided solutions to problems rather than let the children draw their own conclusions. 2. Bradley ripped up his book report in response to the anger he felt when he learned that Carla would be leaving. Confusing her involuntary transfer with abandonment, Bradley reverted to his former bad behavior. 3. Bradley received a gold star from his teacher for the book report that Carla had retrieved from the garbage and taped together. Bradley was still too upset by Carla's imminent departure to appreciate his first gold star. 4. Bradley tried to write a letter to Carla at his father's suggestion to express his regret for not coming to say goodbye to her before she left. 5. Jeff patiently explained to Bradley what he was to expect at the birthday party. He also counseled him on what to wear. Once they arrived at the door, he signaled Bradley when he made inappropriate remarks. 6. It was clear that Bradley had a successful experience at the party when the girls competed for his attention, he won the top prize for games, and his gift was received well. 7. It was clear that Carla was a successful counselor when Bradley revealed in his letter that he was doing well academically and that he was able to relinquish one of the toy animals upon which he had been dependent.

LEARNING LINKS